GIFT FOR THE AGES
LOVE, FAITH, AND POETRY

Yasmin Senturias, MD

Copyright © 2024 Yasmin Senturias

All rights reserved.

ISBN:979-8-9912400-1-7

DEDICATION

I dedicate this book to my husband, Michael who has always believed in me as a person, a doctor, and a poet; to my son, Micah, who is himself a poet and my beloved inspiration, encourager, and challenger; to my brother, Troi, whose travels inspired me to see more worlds than meet the eye; and to my parents, Al and Linda Senturias, who have nourished me in the love of the arts, poetry and life.

INVITATION

In this poetry collection, I invite readers on a journey through life's most treasured moments. The verses within celebrate the profound beauty of family, the enduring warmth of love, and the unadulterated joy hidden in everyday life. I look forward to sharing the beauty I have found in the various seasons of my life. Through these lines of poetry, I hope to embrace you with the love, faith and resilience that bind us all.

ACKNOWLEDGMENTS

Many thanks to everyone who has been a part of my life and who has been instrumental in this book's creation through their presence, nurturing, and love. I hope that the blessings you have bestowed upon me will multiply in your lives and in the lives of everyone you encounter. Most of all, I give praise and thanks to God, who has given me this life and the opportunity to live it out creatively and joyfully.

Psalm 139:14 NRSV
I praise you, for I am fearfully and wonderfully made.
Wonderful are your works; that I know very well.

CONTENTS

CHAPTER 1: FAITH, HOPE AND JOY 1
  Happiness 2
  Gratitude 3
  Daring 4
  Joy 5
  In the Potter's Hands 6
  On Faith 7
  Mountaintop 8
  After 9
  Sunflower Fields 10
  Waiting 11
  Positivity 12
  When in the Crossroads 13
  Sonnet of Gratitude for Fifty Years 14
  Loaves and Fishes 15
  Turning Half a Century 16
  Blessings 17
  On Friendship 18
  In God's Hands 20
  Sunset 21
  We Are Here 22
  Affirm everyone 23
  Heal Thyself 24
  New Year 25
  Not Strangers 26

CHAPTER 2: LOVE 27
  Love 28
  We've Travelled Together 29
  Car Rides with You 30
  When God Gave You To Me 31
  Love Makes You Melt 32
  What is love? 33
  Us 35

For Our 21st 36
That You May Be Rooted and Grounded in Love 37
22nd 38
Falling Leaves 39
A Mother's Love 40
Through 41
Sleepless Nights 42
The New and The Old 43
Mothers 45

CHAPTER 3: NATURE 46
Family Hikes Up the Crowders Mountain 47
Hiking In Late Winter 49
The Making of an Igloo 50
Alive 51
Mount Mayon 52
Sunset at the Beach 53
Love For Flowers 54

CHAPTER 4: PLACES 55
A Maldivian Sunset 56
A Sunny Day in Maldives 57
Saint-Saphorin 58
Lake Brientz 60
In London's Heart 61
The Parthenon 62

CHAPTER 5: FAMILY 63
Childhood Memories 64
Lullaby 66
My Mother's Love 67
Ode to Fathers 68
Father's Day 69
A Sonnet for My Love 70
For Mom and Dad's 43rd Anniversary 71
Our Little Family 73
From the Very First 74
A Boy of Two 76
At Three He Loved Thomas the Tank Engine 77

A Sonnet for Our Son on His 18th Birthday 79
For Your 19th Birthday (A Pandemic Birthday) 80
Twenty-One 81
Sonnet for Mom's 73rd Birthday 82
Honoring Mothers 83
What Will the World Do Without Mothers? 84
Mothers 85
Serving with Heart 88
Celebrating Fathers 89
The World Traveler 90
A Sonnet for My Brother 91
Belated Happy Birthday 92
The Most Beautiful Woman 93
Sonnet for Our Parents' 50th Anniversary (12/24/20) 94
Ageless 95
Sewing Machine 96
Her hands 97
The Most Beautiful Baby 98
The Monkey, the Turtles and the Stories My Grandfather Told Me 99
Chompy 100

CHAPTER 6: COUNTRY, STRUGGLE AND IDENTITY 101

My Body Is Changed Forever 102
Ang Makapiling Ka 104
To Be With You 105
For Women Minorities in the 21st Century 106
An Ode to the City I Live In 107
Insomnia 108
Twenty-Five Years 109
Original Filipino Version: Dalawamputlimang Taon 112
Batch '98 114
Broken Dreams 116
I Have a Vision of a World 117
About the Author 119

CHAPTER 1

FAITH, HOPE AND JOY

"She smiles like she has lived through several lifetimes of joy.
She challenges the world as if she has never been told no.
I wish I could match her love, but the love of my
mother is unmatchable."

Micah Baldonado

You give me so much joy, my son!

HAPPINESS

Happiness is a wildflower,
That some people ignore,
That some trample on.
For it is not majestic,
Unlike the royal rose,
Nor is it exquisite
As the lovely orchid.
But it blooms freely,
Spreads across fields,
Brightening the countryside,
Refreshing the atmosphere.
If we do not change our pace
And stop to wonder about the wild blooms
That abound in our hearts,
That make us sing with gladness,
We will never own a petal
Nor cherish a single stem of this flower.
If we never stop and wonder
About the simple things in life,
If we cease to rejoice
In the little that we have,
We will never be happy.
For happiness is everywhere,
But we all must open our eyes
Wide enough.

GRATITUDE

No one is promised
One more year, month, or minute.
So, when we behold the shadow
Of a new year,
We can't help
But celebrate life
And all its vicissitudes.
So, we affirm aging—
Achy bones, stiff joints,
Facial lines and hand wrinkles.
We rejoice not in riches,
But in the knowledge
That there are people
Who love us,
And whom we love,
And that we make a difference.
We reflect that little things—
Good or bad—
Really matter.
We realize we get wiser
When we fall
And more gracious
When we help someone up.
We fight for what is right,
And we live with the consequence.
And we realize that
Kindness is its own reward,
That gratitude is its own gift.

DARING

Throw caution to the wind, unfurl your sails,
The sea of life, with open arms, does call,
As whispers from the wind tell timeless tales,
It's time to journey forth and give your all.
The joys of life await, don't hesitate,
This is the moment, seize the golden chance,
Bold and unbound, your fate you shall create,
The ocean is your stage, your grand romance.
Yours is the sea, a boundless, endless blue,
With courage, move ahead, embrace the day,
In daring dreams, your spirit shall renew,
No fear, no doubt, let all that drift away.
With winds of change, you'll chart your destiny,
Embrace the sea of life, forever free.

JOY

If I could distill the joy in the universe
To bring it to you—
On your lap, on your face,
Like a gentle mist,
Or a bouquet of flowers,
Every second,
Every minute,
And every hour,
I would run for miles
With all my power—
To bring you happiness
Like a warm embrace,
Like a gentle bower.

IN THE POTTER'S HANDS

In hands of artists, clay doth life receive,
Molded and shaped, from earth's cold, formless sleep.
In silent dance, the steady fingers seek
To touch, and mold, new vessels to conceive.
To bring to life beneath the artist's gaze,
Vessels from dust, with tender care are born.
Fashioned and turned, in the wise Potter's ways,
From humble clay, new beauty will adorn.
These fragile creations, that would often break,
Akin they are to life's ephemeral day.
Thus, Jeremiah's ancient verse imparts
A lesson deep in God's creative heart.
In every turn of life, we thus are shaped—
Our fragile, fleeting selves, God liberates.

"The word that came to Jeremiah from the Lord: "Come, go down to the potter's house, and there I will let you hear my words." So I went down to the potter's house, and there he was working at his wheel. The vessel he was making of clay was spoiled in the potter's hand, and he reworked it into another vessel, as seemed good to him."
Jeremiah 18:1-4

ON FAITH

From the vast and deep valley of despair,
In shame, in grief, when skies are overcast,
When crushing heartache fills the heavy air,
And all seems lost, and hope is fading fast.
One thing endures, unyielding through it all,
And that is faith, a beacon in the night.
In faith, we find the strength to still stand tall,
Believing in the Unseen, taking flight.
The Comforter, Creator, we embrace.
With faith, we dream and dare to reach for stars.
In faith, we find our purpose and our place,
Invisible yet real, with no holds barred.
Through sorrow's depth, in faith, we find our way,
In faith, we glimpse the dawning light of day.

MOUNTAINTOP

It's true.
The wind blows harder at the top.
But never mind,
Don't ever stop
Pursuing all your dreams
With everything that means.
Don't you lose heart—
That distant star
Is closer than it seems.

AFTER

The rains, they come and go.
The rivers ebb and flow.
The seasons always change.
Well, nothing stays the same.
The storms, they often pass.
The waves, they never last.
However long's the night,
The morning brings us light.

SUNFLOWER FIELDS

I am making a run for the sunflower fields
On a hot summer day,
Sweat pouring down my face.
I will not mind the heat
Because when my feet
Land in that meadow
Of vibrant green and spectacular yellow,
I will breathe in contentment
And the bliss of existence.
The most cheerful of greetings
Will be mine for the taking,
And likewise, for the making.
Oh, field where joy blossoms and hopes come alive—
Bring me back to you, and let my spirit thrive!

WAITING

A river of tears surrounds me as I tread,
My mind and body weary, my soul beaten down,
My flooded eyes, with sorrow overspread,
Can't glimpse the path where hope may yet be found.
I trudge along in silence, in ah… soul-wrenching pain,
The rising air, a stifling, heavy shroud,
As sun descends and darkness is displayed,
I walk unyielding, under nighttime's cloud.
With patient heart, I wait for morning's grace,
For God's love unfailing to shine through,
In darkest hours, I find a steadfast place,
Believing that His light will still pierce through.
Through tears and shadows, faith remains, unbroken,
In quiet hope, God's love is softly spoken.

"Remembering mine affliction and my misery…it is of the
Lord's mercies that we are not consumed,
because his compassions fail not.
They are new every morning: great is thy faithfulness."
Lamentations 3:19,22, 23 KJV

POSITIVITY

Well, that did not go so well.
But I'd rather not dwell
On what went wrong.
It won't take long
For me to see
Life's tapestry
Weaving me in
Through thick and thin.
In moments dark,
When hope seems stark,
The brilliant sky I witness.
The clouds, they leave me breathless.
Some clouds of doubt
Weave in, weave out
In the ever-changing weather,
But still, I see the silver lining.
Behind that cloud—
The sun is shining.
My hope, my joy, is endless!

WHEN IN THE CROSSROADS

When in the crossroads of life you stand
Unsure of your bearings, of just where you might land,
Remember your calling, you've got to go back,
Think of what you have now, and not what you lack.
When the hurdles are many, the choices seem few,
Decide with courage, let your hope renew!
The road may be rugged,
The path may be steep,
But your courage will bring you
To the place that you seek.
With a mind that is true,
And a faith that endures
Your hard work, it will lead you
To a victory sure.

SONNET OF GRATITUDE FOR FIFTY YEARS

In gratitude for reaching half a century,
I will be ever thankful for each day.
Each breath from now until eternity,
I'll live, I'll laugh, I'll learn, I'll work, and pray.
Then humbly, I will ask the Lord for courage
And grace to face the challenge of each day,
And joy to share that someone I'll encourage,
And faith to light the path and lead the way.
I'll dream new dreams and pair them all with action.
I'll climb the mountains I intend to climb.
I'll share my hopes and I will share my vision.
I'll love with all my heart and all my mind.
In gratitude, my voice in song I'll raise
A hymn of joy, a song of grateful praise.

Psalm 139:13-14 ESV
"For you formed my inward parts;
you knitted me together in my mother's womb.
I praise you, for a I am fearfully and wonderfully made.
Wonderful are your works; my soul knows it very well."

LOAVES AND FISHES

A woman named Egeria,
A native of Iberia,
Told us that in Tabhgha,
Or in Hebrew, Ein Sheva,
There's a church that enshrines
A memory sublime…
The Lord's miracle to behold
Multiplying fish and loaves.
'Twas the kindness of a child
That made our loving Savior smile.
Faith and hope they did abound,
With food enough to go around.
Those hearts and minds a fertile ground,
Those hungry souls, Christ's word they found.

John 6:9, 11
"There is a boy here her's womb.

I praise you, for a I am fearfully and wonderfully made.
Wonderful are your works; my soul knows it very well."

TURNING HALF A CENTURY

Fifty years is a long time,
Though it seemed to have happened
In a blink of an eye,
In a heartbeat—
Musings and contemplations,
Dreams and inspirations,
Mysteries and discoveries,
Melodies and harmonies,
Road trips and plane rides,
Mountain and seaside,
Sunset and sunrise,
Starlight and sunlight,
Memory and oblivion…
Nothing happens in a vacuum.

BLESSINGS

May God smile upon you.
May God open up the skies to bless you.
May you find joy in the everyday.
May joy find you and in your heart stay.
Blessings of good health and hearty laughter
Be with you today and ever after.

ON FRIENDSHIP

When friendship's roots run deep,
The ground beneath is blessed.
And though the earth still sleeps,
It boldly will profess:
Spring soon will come!
Flowers will bloom!
Winter soon will end!
And when we meet again,
We will pick up
Exactly where we ended
From way, way, way back when.

Thank you to my dear friends who have been there for me throughout the years—from my UPIS batchmates, especially TYNGE (Myling, Carina, Marla, Jem, Mona, Rhon, Anne, Tere, Te, Arni, Bey, Roanna, Joey, Jemma, Malyn), PLB (Shelly, Manny, Tessa, Leizl, Abi, Tanya, Yas, Alvin, Eric), and the Intar Tough 40, to UPCM '95 and UP PGH Pediatrics Ganda '98. I'm grateful for all my dormmates (Tessa, Joy, Hazel, Donna, Frankie, Janette, Awit), childhood friends (Ate Tata, Ate Edith, Vicki, Janine, Mang, Carol), and church friends from Citadel, Cosmopolitan Church, Ellinwood, UCCP Paradahan, UCCP Kawit, Signal Village Church, Center Church, Fairlawn West, Holy Covenant, and Emanuel Reformed. I am very grateful for friends and colleagues from UPCM, Yale, Akron Children's, WCEC, Atrium, CDC, AAP, and SDBP, as well as for FASD champions of all ages. Thank you to my friends who have prayed for me through cancer and beyond (Monique, Sunny, Trish, Cristy, Ate Darl, Kuya Dan, Wendy, Carrie, Anne, Suzanne, Bret, Cynthia D, Cynthia G) and all the friends I've met along life's path.

IN GOD'S HANDS

Teach me, dear Lord, to count the fleeting days.
Infuse my heart with wisdom's guiding light.
In steadfast faith, your Word I shall obey,
For in its truths, your reign is vast and bright.
I've witnessed virtue's bloom and shadow's blight,
Yet 'neath your wings, unmatched is your defense.
In every trial, you've shielded us with might,
Guarding your people with strength and recompense.
So let me learn to treasure each sunrise,
To seek your guidance in this earthly haze.
With numbered days, may wisdom's beacon rise,
As in your grace, my heart forever stays.
In you, O Lord, my faith shall firmly stand,
With love and grace, I'll heed your guiding hand.

"So, teach us to number our days that we may
get a heart of wisdom"
Psalm 90:12

SUNSET

There is a sense in which
We can analyze a sunset--
The brightness and the hues,
The richness of the views,
And yet not understand it,
Nor unveil it or define it.
The sun going down
By those mountains,
Or the oceans,
Framed by clouds--
Those gaseous curtains,
And by memories
Rich and certain.

WE ARE HERE

We are here
To preserve the earth and sky and sea.
We are here
For the future of humanity.
We are here
So we all can eat and drink and breathe.
We are here
To make all the world a sanctuary.
We are here
To preserve the air our children breathe.
We are here
To plant, not to cut down the trees.
We are here
To call for all the wars to cease.
We are here
To have a future bright and free.
We are here
So that nations as one will be.
We are here
So that freedom reigns across the sea.
We are here
For the future of humanity.
We are here
For the future of this world we see.
We are here.

AFFIRM EVERYONE

Not everyone
Has someone
Who will be by their side
Through tumultuous tides,
Who will reach out to say
You're all right, you're ok.
And you may have been there before.
So, affirm each one
As a daughter or son
Or a loved one.
What a joy you'll bestow
When in kindness you go
To lend an ear
Or helping hand
And be someone
Who understands,
Speaking words of affirmation--
Giving hope and inspiration.

HEAL THYSELF

Physician, heal thyself, we hear.
But the wounds are deep,
And the battle is near
And dear to our hearts.
We learned the healing arts,
But somehow have forgotten how
To heal ourselves…we suffer now
From stress and strain,
Heartaches and pain.
What will it take for us to learn
We do not always need to burn
While giving light?
It's worth the fight
To make things right.
The healing process needs to start.
Don't you lose faith,
Don't you lose heart.

NEW YEAR

The new year dawns with hope so bright,
A fresh beginning, thoughts like morning's dew,
May it give us renewed insight,
To dreams and goals, may it reveal what's true.
Infuse in us a fresh determination,
A deep desire to love, to care, to soar,
As new horizons beckon, revelation,
In cherished moments, recognize what's more.
With God's grace, we'll strive to do our best,
For families, communities near and far.
As partners, we'll embark on this great quest,
To heal the world, beneath our Guiding Star.
So let the new year's hope and promise unfurl,
With hope and strength, we aim to change the world.

NOT STRANGERS

We the people of this beautiful earth,
Regardless of language, culture, or place of birth,
Are bound by our common humanity,
Our hopes, dreams, strengths, and frailties.
Inextricably linked one to the other—
Not strangers… we are sisters and brothers.

Photo taken of the Palais des Nations
Geneva, Switzerland

CHAPTER 2

LOVE

And now these three remain: faith, hope and love.
But the greatest of these is love.

1 Corinthians 13: 13

LOVE

Love is that coffee you make,
And the warmth that comes with it.
It is the smile that lights up your face
Seeing me when I awake,
Hair all tousled, without makeup,
How your eyes still light up.
How you have been brave to taste
All the dishes that I make.
It is the way that you remember
Stories I told you from whenever.
Upholding vows made with one breath,
Whether in sickness or in health.
It is the dinners in candlelight,
Silent musings in the night.
It is that gentle hug and firm embrace,
And all the memories they create.
Love's how you've made my dreams take flight.
Yes, you are my strong and silent knight!

WE'VE TRAVELLED TOGETHER

We've travelled together
For thousands of miles,
Rough roads, smooth ones,
Rare frowns, many smiles.
You bring us to places
You've been to before,
And show us the beauty
Of less and of more.
It's not just the endpoint
Of trips we go through,
It's always the journey,
The journey with you.

CAR RIDES WITH YOU

Front row,
Morning glow,
Sunlight--
Warm and bright.
Shielding my face
From all the light,
Singing along
To all those songs
We sung
When we were young…
I will never be blue
On car rides with you.

WHEN GOD GAVE YOU TO ME

When God gave you to me, the mountains danced.
The flowers laughed in glee, and church bells rang.
The trees they danced, rejoiced in pure delight.
The sky was kind, the sun above shone bright.
You've filled my life with kindness and with grace.
Your thoughtfulness and sweetness still amaze.

May God continue to give you wisdom, courage,
faith, hope, love, health and joy for the living of
your days. We love you!!!

Psalm 16:11
Thou dost show me the path of life;
in thy presence there is fulness of joy,
in thy right hand are pleasures for evermore.

LOVE MAKES YOU MELT

Love makes you melt—
Like butter on toast,
Marshmallows you roast,
Chocolate on a hot day,
Snow on a sleigh,
Ice cream on your face,
On a hot sunny day.

WHAT IS LOVE?

For My Husband:
Valentine's Day 2014

What is love?
Is it communing with the mind
Or speaking to the heart of another
Or letting the eyes speak for themselves?
Is it in a bouquet of flowers
Or sweet treats in a box
Or a fresh, mailed letter?
Is it in the soul of laughter
Or in the flowing of tears
Shed from one to another?
Is it in rhythm of dance
Or in the cadence of tunes
Of joy or of sadness?
Is it in a filling meal
Prepared by busy hands,
And served with affection?
Is it in a simple touch,
A kiss after a long day
Or a warm bear hug?

Is it knowing you are thought of?
Is it knowing that you are valued?
Is it knowing you are loved?
All of these I've seen.
You have given.
We have shared.
But today I saw love
In the snowstorm,
In the man who walked eight miles
To get lifesaving medicine
And flowers
For me...
I cannot thank you enough.
I may never fully understand love.
But today, again, you've shown me.
And that is enough.

US

We've come a long, long way, beloved one.
We've seen so many moons and setting suns.
We've come a long way from where we begun,
Through roads, through life, through where the river runs.

My soul's companion, the half that makes me whole.
Your heart you gave, since when my heart you stole.
The passing of the days, the endless tides,
Were well spent, love, with you all by my side.

Your faith's a beacon— bright'ning many morns.
Your love's an anchor through life's many storms.
Your heart's a sunrise, brilliant in its glow.
Your soul's a stronghold, through life's busy flow.

I celebrate you for the special ways
You filled my world with love through time and space.

FOR OUR 21ST

I thank you for dreams that we dreamed,
And paths that we took--
Detours,
Missteps,
Surprises,
Sunsets,
Sunrises,
Packing,
Unpacking,
Messing,
Organizing.
Oh, the places we've been,
Oh, the places we've known,
But the best of the best
Is your heart — it's my home.

THAT YOU MAY BE ROOTED AND GROUNDED IN LOVE

I bow down and pray
That God, in His infinite wisdom,
Will strengthen your being everyday,
That Christ will dwell in your heart through faith,
That you may be rooted and grounded in love
Of the love of the Father in heaven above.
That you may know its height and depth,
That you will be able to comprehend
Its length and breadth.
And through this that you may know
The love of Christ,
The one who loved purely,
Who sacrificed—
That you may be filled
With the fullness of God.
That you may know
That it is through Him
That we can accomplish
More than we can ask,
Or ever imagine.

Ephesians 4:4-19 NRSV
"I pray that you may be strengthened… through his Spirit and that Christ may dwell in your hearts through faith, as you are being rooted and grounded in love.

22ND

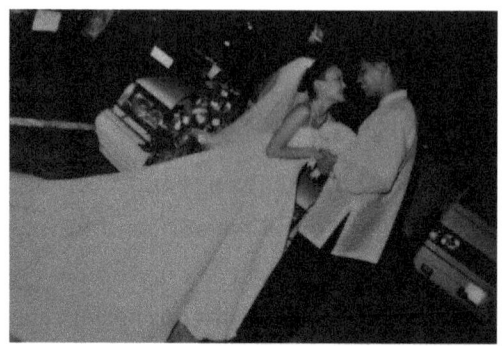

Constantly
Loving me,
Honoring
Our vow.
Patiently,
Graciously,
From then
Until now.
Prayerfully,
Faithfully,
Loving me
Somehow,
Perfectly
Holding me
In the here
And now.

FALLING LEAVES

The poetry of falling leaves
Leaves my soul breathless…
But so does the bliss
Of your hand in mine
And your tenderness.
The glorious color of autumn days
And the air's crispness,
Are best spent in the warmth
Of your strong, strong arms
And your gentleness.

A MOTHER'S LOVE

Some things are absolutely pure,
And that includes a mother's love.
Some things are absolutely sure--
 This is a gift from God above.
I grew up with that love I know,
And I did pray that love to show
My child, my own beloved son,
As stars still shine and rivers run.
A love that has no breaks or bounds—
 This love I have, this love I found.

THROUGH

Love you through mornings,
Love you through nights,
Love you through rainbows,
Love you through strife,
Love you through strong winds,
Love you through calm,
Love you through chaos,
Love you through song,
Love you through good times,
Love you through bad,
Love you through happy,
Love you through sad,
Love you through sickness,
Love you through health,
Love you through low times,
Love you through wealth,
Love you through challenge,
Love you through ease,
Love you through winter,
Love you through spring,
I love you forever…
Through whatever life brings.

SLEEPLESS NIGHTS

Those sleepless nights,
Through teething and feeding,
Congested breathing,
Diaper changing,
Got replaced
With sleepless nights
Of… how are you doing?
Have you been eating?
How are you feeling?
Of books, of school
Of love so fleeting.

THE NEW AND THE OLD

The pandemic did not erase
The seasons or reasons
We gather in this place.
So, we carried on tradition,
Filipino and American
Old and new looms
Woven in the celebration.

So, on Thanksgiving day,
We did our traditional cooking,
Turkey roasting and carving,
Michael setting up the tree
We had since Micah was just three,
Micah putting up the star,
Lighting our hearts, both near and far.
I fulfilled my task— first ornament hung.
With joyful Christmas carols sung

Verses from the bible read,
Reasons for gratitude were said,
And with everyone in place
We bowed our heads, together prayed.
We are thankful for the way,
God gives us all His love and grace.

"Oh, give thanks to the Lord for He is good. His steadfast love endures forever." (Psalm 107)

MOTHERS

Mothers know your heart of hearts,
What's deep inside your soul,
The sorrow that you know,
The pain that helps you grow…
Their wisdom they bestow.
With every single breath,
With every single step,
They aim to care, to bless,
Though there may be missteps,
Their love's there, nonetheless.
Mere words cannot express
Love's depth and breadth.

Proverbs 31:26: "She opens her mouth with wisdom,
and the teaching of kindness is on her tongue."

CHAPTER 3

NATURE

"…Let the earth rejoice; let the sea roar, all that fills it;
let the field exult, and everything in it. Then shall
all the trees of the forest sing for joy."

Psalms 96: 11-12

FAMILY HIKES UP THE CROWDERS MOUNTAIN

Crowder's mountain is our family's delight,
With Michael, Micah, Chompy, under skies ever bright,
Steep trails, rough paths and many rugged steps,
Kept us challenged, kept us centered on our every ascent.

The trees adorned the path of sweet nature's wonderland,
Birds in flight above, ah, a swift tranquil band.
With silence so profound, our spirits gently soared,
In this wilderness, we felt safe and restored.

Those hewn rocks, a mystery, and truly works of art,
Carved by nature, they speak to the mind and the heart,
From their lofty perch, a grandeur we could see--
Charlotte and beyond, a city, wild and free.

Thirty miles away, in your embrace we'd roam,
With nature's chorus as our true and cherished home,
Chirping birds, our heartbeats, sweat shining on our skin,
Amidst ferns and ladybugs, life's beauty lies within.

Logs to cross, memories etched in stone,
In those hikes, our family's love for nature grown,
Crowder's Mountain, dear treasured, loving space
For each adventurous step and for every wild embrace.

HIKING IN LATE WINTER

Hiking in late winter's icy air,
With hopes of spring, my spirit takes its flight,
My heart aflutter, nature's love affair,
In search of warmth and nature's pure delight.
My soul does thirst for life's renewing grace,
To wander 'round rough trails, I gladly roam,
In every step, a new world we embrace,
And hope life wakes up from its winter's home.
Ready for new life, through darkness drear,
Along the rugged paths where wonders play,
Before we know, the winter disappears,
As sun and blossoms greet the light of day.
In nature's arms, where dreams and trails align,
We find our hope, our hearts and souls entwined.

THE MAKING OF AN IGLOO

First, you'll need a lot of snow,
And little hands and feet that go
With singular resolve to make
A half-sphere makeshift snow abode.

ALIVE

The fresh smell of sprouted herbs
Coming from my little garden,
Thriving with a little rain,
A little dirt, a lot of sun.
Despite not having a green thumb—
They just grow, my little ones.
Determined to live,
Determined to thrive—
Our gentle Mother Earth
Kept these herbs alive.

MOUNT MAYON

Photo courtesy of Troi Senturias

Fierce in your beauty,
Oblivious to the sorrows
Of the people at your feet—
Or have you known more sorrow
In your long life
Than you care to enlighten us with?
What have you seen
For your anger to seethe?
What we see is your molten anger,
And furious, exploding rocks,
Always locked within,
Always threatening to break free!
Beneath that perfect cone,
Picturesque in its quietude,
Beneath the fantastic sky,
What secrets do you hide
So fiercely locked within,
Poised to strike at whim?

SUNSET AT THE BEACH

Part 1

Bare feet and bare legs

In the cold ocean water

Seeking the warm sand.

Part 2

Beauty, oh, beauty

Pink, blue, red, majestic sky

And I—swept to shore.

LOVE FOR FLOWERS

Unbridled beauty
Fragrance and colors so bold
A balm for the soul.

Bathe me with color
Visions of red, peach, purple
My soul's enraptured.

CHAPTER 4

PLACES

"Oh, the places I've been! Oh, the places I've known!
But the best of the best is your heart, it's my home."

-Yasmin Senturias

A MALDIVIAN SUNSET

Photo courtesy of Troi Senturias

Surely, I have seen such rich colors,
Such vibrant hues,
From sunsets back home and in other lands,
But the pinks and the purples,
Amidst this lush verdant landscape,
Framing the white sand,
Salty air and placid sea,
Waves lapping gently on the shore,
Beckon my senses, my thoughts and my dreams,
From the rough and tumble
Of my everyday life
To this poetry of the sky
In this island paradise.

A SUNNY DAY IN MALDIVES

'Neath picture perfect skies,
Sunlight gentle on the eyes,
I sat on a ladder
On a house built on stilts,
And my feet touched water,
Washing sand off my toes,
Washing off all my woes…
Fresh smell of sea foam,
Somehow, I felt at home.

SAINT-SAPHORIN

Mist and clouds over Saint-Saphorin,
By the villas of Lavaux-Oran,
Terraced vineyards by the lake,
Cautious steps we had to take
To get to higher ground.
Chiseled wonder I have found.
Terraced vineyards spread for miles,
My eyes, they feasted, but in a while,
Bigger steps we had to take
Raindrops chasing in our wake.

Then seeking refuge from the rain,
Walking down that wet terrain,
We saw a steepled sanctuary,
A haven for us, folks ordinary.

Within those walls, the warmth we sought
Was found, with it some dryness brought.
Inside the church, 'twas almost black
But for the light stained windows had
Allowed to enter in,
These hallowed walls within.
Then gentle music played,
Beautiful sounds were made,
A prelude played and carols sung,
Within our hearts, church bells we rung.

LAKE BRIENTZ

The turquoise lake beckons,
As in a song,
A tranquil haven
For which I long.
In the heat of the sun,
And amid the throng.
The fragrant smell
Of the summer breeze
And the clouds overhead
Put me at ease.
There's a sense of excitement,
There's a sense of bliss,
Amid mountain grandeur
In a place such as this.

IN LONDON'S HEART

In London's heart, where history resides,
Buckingham Palace, so grand and full of grace,
The guards that barely blink, the gates that open wide,
Where royalty still holds a cherished place.
Big Ben— historic —standing tall and bright,
A beacon in the city's endless night,
Its face does gleam, a timeless, steadfast sight,
Guiding Londontown with silent might.
St. Paul's Cathedral, steeped in history's lore,
A sacred space, its dome so high above!
From old Tower Bridge, sweet views we did explore.
On London Bridge our hearts did swell with love--
In twenty-thirteen, when with Uncle Troi we roamed,
Through London's treasures, memories we've owned,
From Shakespeare's stage to fish and chips delight,
In this great city, our hearts and minds took flight.

THE PARTHENON

Oh, Parthenon, you stand in time's embrace,
Ruins and columns, rugged, ancient face.
A beacon on the hill, a hope sublime,
A citadel of old, democracy's shrine.
Pericles, the statesman, bold and wise,
Espoused democracy and women's rights.
Equality, a concept age-old and true,
Discovered long before our modern view.
Hunter-gatherers, consensus reached of yore,
In families, tribes, communities and more.
Even Phoenicians, in their distant days,
Held assemblies, to build harmonious ways.
Oh, Parthenon, your light still shines so bright,
A testament to principles through the night
In ancient times, your wisdom did implore,
To shape a world for freedom evermore.

CHAPTER 5

FAMILY

"The love of family warms the heart, refreshes the soul,
enlivens the spirit and makes us whole."

Yasmin Senturias

CHILDHOOD MEMORIES

Someone said life can be summed up
In a few moments, a few memories.
Dad, on Father's Day,
I remember such golden memories.
Climbing up mountains,
Or maybe they were just hills,
But to me they were thrilling,
And we were always singing.
Tales of struggle
Under starlight
I loved to hear them
Through the dark night.
And living days of struggle—
Christmas in the picket line...
Among other things.

Hide and seek while blindfolded
Was a game that we played...
With Troi and Mom I remember
Those moments together.
Heart to heart talks
And fiery speeches,
Fighting injustice
Standing for the weak,
Serving God and serving others.
These moments molded me.
To the person I set out to be.

LULLABY

Because my Dad sang to me,
I felt the calm
Of my Mother's womb,
Of my lost paradise.
Because Dad sang to me,
I felt the calm
That music brings,
And it is where
My being sings.

MY MOTHER'S LOVE
March 15, 2021

My mother's love runs deep, this much I know,
As strong as oceans roar, as rivers flow.
And when the storms do rock the ground below,
I find her hand in mine, not letting go.
I know in life there are uncertainties;
Yes, there are things that we will never know.
But I have learned her love will always be
A place where I can be, where I can go.
Through you, I learned the fierce and steady love
Of a strong mother and our God above.

ODE TO FATHERS

Hail to all fathers who on earth do dwell,
Hail to those living in our hearts as well,
For each of them has given us a part
Of kindness, goodness, dwelling in their hearts.
For you who've given us a happy childhood,
Of memories to cherish until adulthood,
Who nourished us with food and love and laughter,
And faith to live both now and ever after,
Your loving family gratefully give to you,
Our joyful voices, songs and verses, too.

FATHER'S DAY

You were there…
When he was running in the playground
Or chasing after pigeons,
You never let him skin his knee,
Yet you let him run so free.
Well, you saw his first steps,
Videotaped those for me.
Where he forgot that gravity
Used to bring him to his knees.
You taught him to persevere
In tennis, in music, in life.
You taught him to be resilient
Through hardships, failure and strife.
You taught him to speak his mind
And yet be gentle, and yet be kind.
You taught him to have faith,
To be steadfast and to pray.
And today we greet you:
A Happy Father's Day!

A SONNET FOR MY LOVE

Steadfast, stalwart, bold, and iron-willed
Who though keeps silent, knows just when to speak.
A puzzle solver, practical and skilled,
Tall and handsome with a definite mystique.
You are diligent, caring, faithful, and sweet.
A loving husband, father, brother, son,
Enduring faith, justice, and truth you seek,
Through thick and thin, you truly are the one.
God bless you, guide you, each step of the way.

FOR MOM AND DAD'S 43RD ANNIVERSARY

Forty-three years ago,
At a church in the city,
You were married
Bright and early.
It was the 24th of December,
A lovely day to remember,
With Christmas just a day away.
One Christmas (and two weeks) later,
Came a daughter
And summers after, a son.
You gave them
A happy childhood,
Fondly they remember…
Family gatherings, church meetings,
Fun outings, games and singing,
Teaching and talking,
Prayer and blessing.
You were engaged
(And in a way, we were involved, too)
In worship and work,
Advocacy for justice,
Human rights and peace,
Health, healing, wholeness,
Ministry to the marginalized.
Your love for each other
Has always been strong,
True and enduring,
From the very beginning.

You both are
Ever giving,
Ever caring,
Giving light,
Giving sight
To those who are unseeing
Of possibilities unending.

Thank you, Mom and Dad,
For leading us to God, to love
And to paths of service;
For being there for us
And for always loving us.

OUR LITTLE FAMILY

Our journey started in New Haven
In our little slice of heaven.
He was studying Divinity.
I worked in the medical community.
We went to the Church on the Green
Where we felt heard, where we felt seen.
In this sweet place, our little one came.
'Twas where Micah was baptized and named.
He came to us, beautiful and bright,
His sweet voice belting in the night.
He was an easy baby who loved to be held.
For him we sang songs and for him we read.
We let him play and run free
In a multicultural community,
Where the way you look and the way you speak
Is upheld as lovely, true, unique.
In this affirming place, our son took his first steps,
In this loving community, within this simple life we led.

FROM THE VERY FIRST

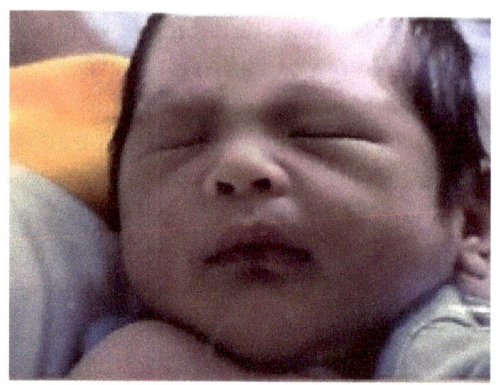

From your first cry,
You have given us joy.
From your first smile,
First laugh, first words, first steps
Our hearts have stirred
And a whole new world was opened.
You had us captive as you left the womb,
Fists up in the air,
Claiming your place in the world
Right there and then.
How did time fly this fast?
From baby bottles and diapers
Train sets and Duplos…
How are we now venturing
Towards college and beyond?

GIFT FOR THE AGES

Today you are sixteen,
Tenacious and outspoken,
Courageous and emboldened,
Seeker of wisdom, seeker of truth.

Let God guide you.
May God hear your prayers
As you stand firmly in God's love
And in ours.
God be with you
As you walk the straight path
And when you blaze through a new one.

A BOY OF TWO

In New Haven town, a boy of two,
With eyes so bright, his world brand new,
His heart was filled with endless glee,
With innocence and curiosity.
Chasing pigeons in the park each day,
In gleeful laughter, he found his way,
With a shovel in the sandbox, he'd play,
Enjoying every minute of every day
At the playground, laughter was shared
With little friends from everywhere,
Multiculturally, joyfully they'd blend,
Creating memories that would never end.
Curiosity filled their eager minds,
A world of wonders for them to find.
In the eyes of this boy, so pure and free,
The wonders of the world, they'll always be
In a red wagon, multicultural and grand,
A world of friendship in his hands.

AT THREE HE LOVED THOMAS THE TANK ENGINE

At three he loved Thomas, that's true,
But Akron's parks held wonders anew,
Exploring nature, we would hike for miles
Though when it seems we've hiked a while
He started to want to be carried on Dad's back
His favorite spot, apart from my lap.
He also loved the zoo, a magical place,
Where penguins waddled with gentle grace,
Their black and white dance, a joyful sight,
In his eyes, all the world was bright.
His friends, Maya, Brighton and Ainsley
Made each day joyful and carefree.
And at Fairlawn church, a place of grace,
We would bring Micah to that sacred space,
In a community that showed God's love
And nurtured his faith in God above.
The library next door was a world to explore,
With shows and stories, he'd long for more.

Ice cream delights in the afternoon sun,
A simple joy, shared by everyone,
Movies were loud, not his cup of tea,
But books, he loved, and for sure, Barney,
Plus Elmo and Clifford, plushies old and new.
Books about animals and yes, earthworms, too.
He liked Dr. Seuss's tales, a world so bright,
The Cat in the Hat was quite a delight.
Connecting all things, like tracks on a train,
From Uncle Troi's wisdom ☺, a lifelong gain,
Foretelling the engineer that he would be,
With an endless supply of curiosity.

A SONNET FOR OUR SON ON HIS 18TH BIRTHDAY

No more a child, today you are a man
And time, it flew, it sped, it raced, it ran.
We still recall you taking your first steps
To walk this world, its length, its width, its breadth.
I miss the time of bedtime lullabies,
Of chasing birds and worms and butterflies
And soon you're off for bigger, harder, tasks
Where is that baby sitting on my lap?
But just today we pause rememb'ring still
Adventures over valley, vale, and hill
And how you've grown, compassionate and wise,
And how our love still glows within your eyes.
There never was a better time to say
May God guide you each step of every day.

FOR YOUR 19TH BIRTHDAY (A PANDEMIC BIRTHDAY)

Oh, what a blessed day, you're now nineteen!
You've conquered freshman year, got your vaccine.
You've got a thousand goals, a million dreams.
Your list of things to do bursts at its seams.
Here's to a blessed year, you are nineteen!
Your last official year to be a teen.
We still recall your first steps, your first smile
Though really, well let's see.. that's been a while!
May God grant you true joy for every day,
Wisdom and love that's in your heart to stay.

TWENTY-ONE

My pride, my joy, you now are twenty-one.
You've had eventful trips around the sun.
You've faced your hurdles squarely in the face,
You met your victories with equal grace.
You've loved both science and psychology,
You've loved math, engineering, poetry.
You've loved music and in it you're free
To feed your soul, your own philosophy.
Your love to break new ground is quite entrenched,
You've taught yourself to speak German and French.
You've taught yourself the language of machines,
Physics and math beyond my grandest dreams.
But most of all, my son, I love your heart
The love you've had in you right from the start.

SONNET FOR MOM'S 73RD BIRTHDAY

In youth a doctor to communities,
With age, a pioneer of diversity,
Speaker, doctor, teacher, emissary
Of words that heal, of deeds done lovingly.
Physician and healthcare visionary,
Woman leader, goal-setter, luminary.
Trailblazer in the field of HIV,
Supporting rights of all humanity.
Beyond this, loving wife and kind mother,
Loving sister, aunt and sweet grandmother
What joy and love in your life we behold
May God keep you healthy, faithful and gold.

"Thanks be to God for His inexpressible gift!" 2 Corinthians 9:15

HONORING MOTHERS

Her lips utter kind words,
Her mind is full of wisdom,
Her heart is full of love,
Her feet, they walk with faith.
She works and perseveres,
She writes and advocates,
She fights for what is right,
She seeks justice and light.
And she gives of herself--
Time, talent, and treasure.
And to us whom she raised,
She gives love without measure.
I honor all mothers.

Proverbs 31:26: "She opens her mouth with wisdom, and the teaching of kindness is on her tongue."

I honor my loving, beautiful, brave and altruistic Mom who has molded me into the Mom and the person I am. I honor you, dear Lola Mama, Lola Petra, and Lola Didang, because your love and care have transcended generations and your children have gone forth to be gentle and loving mothers.

WHAT WILL THE WORLD DO WITHOUT MOTHERS?

What will the world do without mothers?
What will the world do without mine?
She is gentle yet courageous,
She is patient and tenacious.
She embodies integrity,
Bravery and honesty.
She works hard and is persistent,
Dedicated and consistent.
But beyond being a role model,
She is my mother,
Loving and tender,
True encourager.
What will the world do without mothers?
What will I do without mine?

MOTHERS

Today we honor the mothers
Who have been in our lives
Through good and bad weather,
Through triumph or strife.
On this special occasion,
I honor the one
Who in love and compassion
Raised her daughter and son.
You taught us to love,
And our blessings to share
Like our Father above,
Mom, you were always there.
Happy Mother's Day!

We honor all Moms everywhere, those who are here with us and those who have finished their earthly journey. I also honor those who have acted like mothers to us. Honoring my Mom, Lola Mama, Lola Petra, Mama Porette, Aunt Edna, Aunt Luz, Aunt Lita, Aunt Beth, Aunt Mellie, Tita Cheri, Aunt Baby, Aunt Mina, Tita Cho, Aunt Ellie, Tita Cor, Aunt Undette, Aunt Agnes, Aunt Leah, Aunt Enchie, Aunt Eva, Aunt Monina, Aunt Alma, Aunt Lois, Lola Pacing, Lola Lucy, Lola Betty, Lola Mely, Lola Lorie, Ate Beth, Ate Jec and Ate Tata. Thank you!

GIFT FOR THE AGES

SERVING WITH HEART

A Poem for Dad on his 76th birthday

Living with faith,
Serving with heart,
Giving with grace,
Your wisdom impart.
From a lifetime of justice
And fighting for rights,
From preaching to practice,
From darkness to light.

CELEBRATING FATHERS

Strong, faithful, brave, committed, kind, and true,
Our hearts are truly grateful now for you.
This is the day your love we celebrate.
This is the day your labors we will praise!
Children of all ages
We gather here to say:
Thank you for the love you've shared
And Happy Father's Day!

THE WORLD TRAVELER

You came, you saw, you traveled worlds unknown,
And yet you never were so far from home.
Unwav'ring in your love of family,
You found ways to reach out across the seas.
Your giving ways in truth set you apart
For you sincerely give— straight from the heart.
Your quest for justice truly does inspire,
Your quest for truth is something to admire.
You know how to relax, re-energize,
To gaze at ocean foams, the earth, the skies.
You make life fun for all those you hold dear,
May you be blessed today and through the years.

A SONNET FOR MY BROTHER

You have a loving heart, a caring soul.
You seek a world, that's just and fair and whole.
You shine with kindness, generosity.
You make the world a better place to be.
You've travelled far and wide, this much is true.
I have a ways to go, before I do.
But in those many times we've journeyed through,
So good to roam and see this world with you.
Though many miles are wedged between us two,
And many storms have come, and trials true,
It gives me strength to know I have a brother
Who'll stand by me through wind and fire and water.
I pray to God for you this joyful day
That God bless you in each and every way.

BELATED HAPPY BIRTHDAY

So, your birthday has passed,
I'll be greeting you last.
Though the order does matter,
You'll be thanking me after,
'Twill make our bond stronger,
To make your birthday last longer!
To my brother, my friend:
May that day never end.
May you feel the joy of your birth,
For your every day on this earth.

THE MOST BEAUTIFUL WOMAN

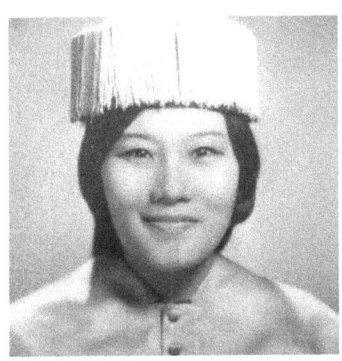

My mother is the most beautiful woman in the world.
Her eyes are bright,
Her smile so warm,
And her heart is pure as gold.
Out of her heart
Comes beautiful things.
She is masterful
At loving and giving.
Her faith is strong,
Her love is pure,
And the oil of service
She generously pours.
My mother is the most beautiful woman in the world.

SONNET FOR OUR PARENTS' 50TH ANNIVERSARY (12/24/20)

From that first moment that these two souls met,
It was electric, joyful, Heaven-sent.
A hand on hand was truly heart on heart,
From that first moment never then to part.
A love so true has never yet been made--
A blooming flower never meant to fade.
Five decades spent in love and prayer and growth,
Five decades being true to that their oath--
To love and to hold from that very day
That two hearts were joined in a blessed way.

To love, to cherish in sickness and health,
To love in truth, in poverty or wealth.
We honor fifty years of love and faith.
Grateful for your love, we all now celebrate!

AGELESS

Lilacs and diamonds
Surround you in your soft throne.
You are always our queen--
So regal and serene.
You reached the age
When you are fully
Lauded for longevity,
Beauty, grace and purity
Molded by adversity…
Brilliantly you shine!
A vision so sublime—
Lilac bouquets so endless
And you, beautiful, wise, ageless.

SEWING MACHINE

For My Lola, Builder of Dreams

You sewed not for a living
But for all to live well--
Children, grandchildren,
For those who with us dwelled.
Though your vision blurred with age,
Your mind would never fade,
And the stiffness of your hands
Did not stop you from…
Threading that needle
And mending those seams…
Enchantment creator
And builder of dreams!
In your grit and perseverance
In your faith and sacrifice,
In your acts of love and service,
Our dreams have taken flight.
And though you have left us,
To journey through the night,
Your hands of faith and love
Have brought us to the light.

HER HANDS

The hands that held my feverish face—
Caring hands,
Loving hands,
That cooked and sewed,
With gentleness showed,
That made me hot soup,
When I wasn't feeling good,
Hands that embraced,
Hands that prayed,
And wiped my tears
Away.
Lola, thank you very much.
For all the sacrifices you made,
For the love and care you gave,
We love you deeply,
Forever and always.

THE MOST BEAUTIFUL BABY

**To my Lolo Papa who won the most beautiful baby
contest in St. Lukes Hospital, 1921**

You were the most beautiful baby,
You won that contest fair and square.
They must have seen the glint in your eyes
Foretelling stories you would share.
That baby grew and made us laugh,
And sacrificed on our behalf,
For all his babies to live well,
That their own stories they will tell,
That their own beauty they'll impart.
You gave them wisdom and a heart—
To share, to care, to give their all
In all endeavors big or small.
You lived with humor and with grace,
With love and kindness in your face.
And in your heart, and in your soul
You gave us joy— it was your goal.
You travelled wide, you did your share,
Oh, storyteller extraordinaire!

THE MONKEY, THE TURTLES AND THE STORIES MY GRANDFATHER TOLD ME

You told us that the monkey was speedy and sly.
Since the turtle was slow, he'd be skating by.
Yet the turtle won the race
Patience written on his face.
You told us those stories,
So vivid, so glorious,
In rapid succession,
With vocal expression.
The cadence, the rhythm
And power within
That vivid narration
Inspired the creation,
Of more stories to pass on
To the next generation…
Powered by imagination.

Lolo, you called me "Anyahay." You also inspired me to make sweet, unique nicknames for the people I love. Thank you for the stories and for your beautiful life!

CHOMPY

Loyal friend, loving companion,
A genius when it comes to emotions,
Though you walk not in this mortal coil
You will not fade in oblivion.
You quickly felt at home… and you—
You made us fall in love with you.
You had such beauty in that face.
You ran around with a gentle grace.
Your eyes were soulful and incredibly sweet.
You trotted around with a cheerful beat.
We'd call your name, and you came joyfully.
It was not hard to make you happy.
We thank God for letting you be
A part of our lives,
A part of our family.

CHAPTER 6

COUNTRY, STRUGGLE AND IDENTITY

"To struggle is to live. To live is to struggle. Embrace the struggle."

-Yasmin Senturias

MY BODY IS CHANGED FOREVER

Pain goes away,
Wounds heal,
Scars disappear,
But my body is changed forever.
Something small,
Something insidious
Took over in the fall.
Barely detectable,
But there it was…
Unmistakable…
On the radiographic plate,
The tiny seed
That did invade,
Not palpable but real.

The biopsy said:
Malignant,
Fast growing,
At risk for spreading.
Decisions were made,
All treatments chosen,
Parts of me that had to go
Mapped out
As in a battle plan
To conquer the onslaught,
To abort a siege.

My heart was strong,
My faith untiring,
I walked into the room
Where knives were waiting,
Knowing…

Pain goes away
Wounds heal
Scars disappear
But my body is changed forever.

ANG MAKAPILING KA

Sana madali lamang tumakbo,
Lumipad, lumiban, lumukso—
Upang makapiling ka,
Minamahal kong ina...
Akoy iyong inaruga
Magmula sa pagkabata.
Sa iyong piling unang nagkamalay.
Sa unang mga hakbang ika'y umalalay.
Ikaw ang nagturo ng una kong salita—
Sakdal ng tamis, o sariling wika!
Ako ay naglakbay, nangibang bayan
Walang papantay sa lupa kong sinilangan.
Wala nang iinit pa sa yakap mo.
Walang magmamahal sa'kin ng buong-buo.
Pilipinas, Inang nag-aruga,
Para sa iyo, puso ko ay nangungulila.

TO BE WITH YOU

English Translation of Ang Makapiling Ka

I wish it was easy to run, fly, jump into your arms
Beloved mother,
You took care of me
From my childhood.
In your nurturing arms
I thought my first thoughts
Took my first steps
Spoke my first words
Oh, the sweetness of my mother tongue—
Nothing can compare.
I traveled, and found another country,
Called it my home.
But nothing compares to you, dear mother.
No one will be warmer than your hug.
No one will love me completely.
Dear mother…
Philippines, dear motherland,
My heart longs for you.

FOR WOMEN MINORITIES IN THE 21ST CENTURY

Rosa Parks fought the fight.
For, justice and human rights
And so, here I am, an Asian, a woman,
An immigrant, a first generation American.
I will not give up my seat on the bus—
I have rights just like the rest of us.
As a colored woman, a minority
In this the 21st century
I have had my share
Of decisions unfair
Perhaps by race
Or the color of my face
But I know my place…
And I will be strong.
It will not be long
Till we all unite
And for justice fight
For that day when equality
Is for all a reality.

AN ODE TO THE CITY I LIVE IN

Charlotte, Charlotte from the air,
Green, green, green everywhere.
Of this I am so proud—
Beneath tiny puffs of clouds,
I have a city clean and green,
A haven for the evergreens.
Within city limits are restful lakes
And walking paths we love to take.
In almost any season
There rarely is a reason
Not to walk these gentle miles,
Or breathe in nature for a while.
Some lovely paths I still discover,
Flowers and birds, fir trees and clover.
The air is fresh in these surrounds;
The soil is rich, 'tis fertile ground
To plant some herbs or apple trees
While I enjoy the gentle breeze.
And if I choose, not far from me,
The mountains beckon placidly.

INSOMNIA

My eyes are closed,
My body still,
My mind's still moving
Against my will.
A thousand thoughts
From dawn till dusk,
I long for dreams,
But sleep I must.

TWENTY-FIVE YEARS

Fondly I remember,
It has been since forever—
Our medical school days
And the many ways
We toiled away,
Endless hours of studying
Till the wee hours of morning.
Anatomy, physiology,
Pathology, pharmacology—
Time kept running,
So, of course, we were rushing,
Studying while we ate.
Oh, we had to live in haste;
There was no second to waste.

The hospital beckoned,
With practical lessons
That we needed to learn
For knowledge we yearned--
Normal or pathological,
Medical or surgical.
We needed to be prepared,
For we needed to care
For the young and old,
And every second was gold.
Our teachers inspired us,
And we had it within us,
To be just like them.
To heal just like them,
To master the art
And the science and heart
Of medicine.

GIFT FOR THE AGES

We graduated in '95—
A good year to be alive!
But that was twenty-five years ago.
We have aged that much, I know.
And now here we are,
From both near and far,
Twenty-five years hence,
Seeing you once again
In the midst of a global pandemic
A world ravaged by COVID.
Grateful we have made it through,
I am happy to see all of you.
Through COVID's storm, we've persevered true;
Grateful for this reunion, I am grateful for you!

ORIGINAL FILIPINO VERSION: DALAWAMPUTLIMANG TAON

Words and Music Yasmin Senturias
Arranged by Micah Baldonado
For the 25th Anniversary of UP College
of Medicine Class of 1995

Binabalikan ko....mga alaala—
Anatomiya, pisyolohiya
Hanggang umaga.
Naaalala ko, parang kahapon—
Nagmamadali.
Walang sandaling itinatapon.
At kahit na pagod na pagod,
At oras laging tinatakbo,
Lahat lahat ginagawa ko
Upang maging manggagamot.
Binabalikan ko mga alalala—
Bata matanda kinalalinga
Nitong dalubsaha.
At pinangarap ko, maging dalubhasa…
Sa medisina o siruhiya
Sa puso at diwa.
Ngayong pangarap ay nakamit.
Alam ko na na bawat saglit
Kayo'y karamay at kasama—
Sa hirap… at ginhawa.

Dalawamput limang taon…
Ngayon lang lahat
Magkitkitakita.
Nagpapasalamat ako
Makikita ka
Sa gitna ng pandemiya.
Dalawamputlimang taon…
Nagkakaisa
Sa gitna ng pandemiya.
Dalawamputlimang taon….ngayon!

BATCH '98

When the leaves of this book turn to yellow with age
And the lines on our faces too many to trace
We shall waltz and whirl along memory lane
To that timeless epoch, to that tireless age
Called… pediatric residency.
An eternal domain.

It brings back the child in her mother's embrace
Exhausted from breathing at a tumultuous pace
A sea of faces moving in an effort to save
The life of this child, of this precious babe
And a voice shouting, "Intubate, intubate!"
"Shall we intubate?"

The voices are clamoring as we get the heart rate
Someone calls for a "code," We must resuscitate!"
Yes, those were the days…
We were tired, we were sticky
But at the end of the day,
But we managed to unwind,
Or cry our troubles away.

We had batchmates that fed on laughter
And gave laughter away
Who spiced up our lives
With their eccentric ways
We have quiet and meek ones
Who shocked us some days
We had highly strung ones
Juniors tremblingly obeyed

We had strong willed ones
Seniors could never sway.
And hardworking ones, a lot of us, I'd say
Who burned the midnight oil
In the wards where we stayed
From hour to hour, from hours to days!

It was tough just to write progress notes everyday
Compute catch up rates at an incredible pace
Doing vent taps and lumbar taps and even BMAs,
They were tough…
But with eyes closed
We could hit just the right interspace.
After reading Nelson's at a sleepy snail's pace
We are suddenly jolted, "The exam is today!"
Juggling through differentials
And the FRICHMOND in vain
We freaked out a little
Then partied off the pain.
So, we danced to our music
And we sang through the rain.
In this batch of "Gandas" (literally, beauties)
Everyone had a place
To be their own self
And yet be embraced
By these marvelous people
Whom we called our batchmates!

BROKEN DREAMS

Childhood dreams
Seem to have no place
In the middle of the rubble,
Of the famine that comes with war,
Of the desperation
That comes with a gnawing in the belly,
And the coldness of the air
Through the ripped fabric
Of what was once a pretty dress
That the child wore
To the marketplace,
Or to her place of worship,
Which now is also rubble,
Both the marketplace
And the mosque…
And the church her friend went to.

Where, oh, where did you fly,
My childhood dreams?
I hope I reunite
With you someday.
But first, let me
Find my mother,
And hope she is there
To show me
Where I can get
A bite to eat.

I HAVE A VISION OF A WORLD

I have a vision of a world
Where children are not hungry.
Where they receive what nourishes
The body and the soul,
The curious mind,
The hungry belly,
The lonely heart.
Where there are no shackles
Of poverty, war
Homelessness, pollution, or disease
And that there are medicines,
Food, shelter, and love
To soothe all their ills
That they can confidently move
And live and breathe
And dream.
Oh, what a precious thing
To dream
Of a future…
Beyond the present,
Of need
Of pain
Of suffering.
A future
Where belly laughs
Abound
And blend
With hearty meals
Shared with family
Over mealtime conversations,

Where tears and
Painful memories
Are soothed
Through healing food
And healing words
And healing love

Passed around
From plate to plate,
From soul to soul.
And where the parents,
Cousins, uncles, and aunties
Grandmas and grandpas
Doctors, nurses, teachers
Lived through
A blessed past
And have the breath,
And means,
And health
Of body, mind, and spirit,
To nurture
The inner child
In themselves
And in all of those
Entrusted in their care.
I have a vision
That we all dream this dream
And walk the path
To make this dream
A reality.

ABOUT THE AUTHOR

Dr. Senturias is a developmental and behavioral pediatrician who has been writing poetry all her life. She enjoys singing, writing and traveling but most of all, she enjoys spending time with family.

www.ingramcontent.com/pod-product-compliance
Lightning Source LLC
Chambersburg PA
CBHW071228090426
42736CB00014B/3010